Science in
a Vacant Lot

Science in a Vacant Lot

SEYMOUR SIMON

Illustrated by Kiyo Komoda

THE VIKING PRESS   NEW YORK

For Joyce,
Robert, and Michael

First Edition

Copyright © 1970 by Seymour Simon

First published in 1970 by The Viking Press, Inc.
625 Madison Avenue, New York, N.Y. 10022
Published simultaneously in Canada by
The Macmillan Company of Canada Limited
Library of Congress catalog card number: 78–102924
Printed in U.S.A.

574   1. Nature study
2. Cities

Trade 670–62163–3   VLB 670–62164–1
1   2   3   4   5   74   73   72   71   70

Contents

Exploring Close to Home

A vacant lot isn't really vacant at all. Some people may call it that just because no building stands there. But a vacant lot is full of interesting things to explore. Rocks and trails, animals and plants, even the ground you walk on all have a science story to tell.

You can find out about these stories by being a science explorer. You don't have to travel to the moon or be a deep-sea diver to become a science explorer. You can be an explorer in a nearby vacant lot just by doing what a scientist does.

A scientist observes carefully. He looks at a rock and notices the different materials in it. He feels the rock to see how hard it is and lifts it to see if it is heavy. He listens to the buzzing of an insect and the sound of raindrops. He smells a clump of damp earth and the flowers of a weed. A scientist observes with all his senses.

Sometimes a scientist measures things. He uses a ruler to check on the growth of a plant or the length of an earthworm. He uses a thermometer to tell the temperature in the shade and in the sun. He may also use a scale or a clock or a measuring cup.

A scientist likes to keep track of what he finds out by writing it down. He notes the size of each earthworm that he measures. He makes a drawing of a plant leaf and tries to identify it. He performs experiments, trying out things in different ways. He thinks about his findings and decides what they mean.

But first of all a scientist is curious about the world around him. Many things puzzle him and he begins to search for answers. Often an answer leads to new mysteries, and he continues his search. In a vacant lot you can begin your own explorations in the world of science.

Rocks
and Soil

In a city much of the soil is covered over by concrete or asphalt. But in a vacant lot the soil is at the surface and easy to examine.

Look over the lot. Can you see a path that people take? Perhaps the path is a shortcut from one place to another. Do any plants grow along the path? It seems that most plants won't grow where the soil is trampled down. Even when people stop using the path, it takes some time before plants will grow there.

You can use a pencil to find out how tightly the soil is packed. Make a mark every half-inch along the pencil, starting at the tip. Put the pencil point in the soil at the side of the path. With your palm, press the pencil into the soil as deeply as it will go without hurting your hand. Make a note of the depth. Now try pressing the pencil into the soil every six inches across the width of the path. Record the depth each time.

Notice that the pencil does not go as deeply into the soil in the middle of the path as it does at the path's edges. Walking on soil packs it together. Plants don't grow well in tightly packed soil. But there may be some plants growing in low spots in the path.

Use your marked pencil to test the soil in these spots. Do you expect to find the soil tightly packed there?

Plants are important for soil just as soil is important for plants. Plants protect the soil from being washed away by rainwater. The wearing away of soil is called *erosion*.

When rain falls on bare soil, some of the water flows along the ground. The flowing water picks up bits of soil and moves them from high spots to lower ones. Often you can see gullies where the running water washed the soil away.

Sometimes you may find a rock on a small mound of soil. The rock protected the soil beneath it from being eroded by the force of falling rain. The unprotected soil around the rock was washed away by the raindrops. The rock was left on top of its little hill of soil.

Trees growing on slopes often have bare roots. The roots become exposed when the soil covering them is washed down the slope by rainwater. At the base of a slope, look for rocks and soil that were washed down by the rain.

Lack of enough rain also causes soil erosion in the vacant lot. Without rain, the soil dries out and turns powdery. On a windy day the powdery dust is whipped around in a little whirlwind, and is scattered or eroded. In desert areas of the United States, rapidly whirling dust storms are called "dust devils."

Soil is made up of different sizes and kinds of particles. Some of the particles are too small to be seen without a powerful microscope. These tiny particles are clay. But you can easily see the larger particles of sand in soil.

Another part of the soil is called *humus*. It is made up of roots and decaying plant and animal matter. Humus is usually darker than the rest of the soil. If you put some soil in a can of water, the humus particles often float while the rest of the soil sinks.

10

The top few inches of dark soil contain most of the humus. It is in this topsoil that most plants grow. It may take three hundred years for one inch of topsoil to form in nature.

Dig a hole to see how deep the topsoil is in your vacant lot. Examine the topsoil for bits of decaying roots, stems, and leaves. The lighter-colored soil below the topsoil is called the subsoil. Compare the materials in the subsoil with those in the topsoil. Does the subsoil have any decaying materials in it? What other differences do you see?

You can experiment to find out which part of the soil is better for growing plants. Collect some topsoil in a can and some subsoil in another can. Dampen the soil in each can but not so much that it becomes muddy. Carefully dig up two small plants of the same kind from the lot. Plant one in each of the cans. Put the plants in a spot where they will get some sun each day, and keep the soil moist. Keep a record of what happens to the plants. Which plant do you think will grow better?

You can also perform this experiment by planting two or three lima bean seeds, rather than a plant, in each can. Keep the soil moist as before. Now you can observe how seeds sprout in different soils as well as how plants grow.

You'll find plenty of rocks and stones in a vacant lot. Look at them carefully and see if you can tell whether they are natural or man-made. Man-made rocks include concrete and brick.

Many of the rocks you find in the lot may have been dumped there by man. Others may have been left long ago by flowing water or waves. They are often rounded and smoothed. You can find rounded rocks like these on beaches or in streams.

In northern sections of the United States you may find rocks left behind by rivers of ice called *glaciers*. Glaciers covered many northern parts of the country thousands of years ago during the ice ages. These rocks are sometimes flattened on one side where they have been dragged along by the slowly moving glaciers.

Many rocks are not smoothed or flattened but have sharp edges and rough surfaces. These have broken off from larger chunks of rocks. Examine them carefully. You may see little bits of different materials in the rocks. These materials are called minerals. Rocks are made of minerals. Some rocks are made mostly of one mineral, while other kinds are made of several different minerals.

Try to scratch one rock with another. The rock that is made of the harder minerals will scratch the other. Look at the color of the rock and the size of the mineral particles in it. All these things will help you to identify what kind of rock it is. Once you identify a rock you'll soon learn to recognize others like it whenever you find them.

Here's how to identify some common rocks.

Schist is a scaly rock that often has flakes of a glittery mineral called *mica*. You can see the minerals in schist with your unaided eye. They often form bands of light and darker material. The rock sometimes breaks along these bands.

Granite is a light-colored, speckled-looking rock. The rock is

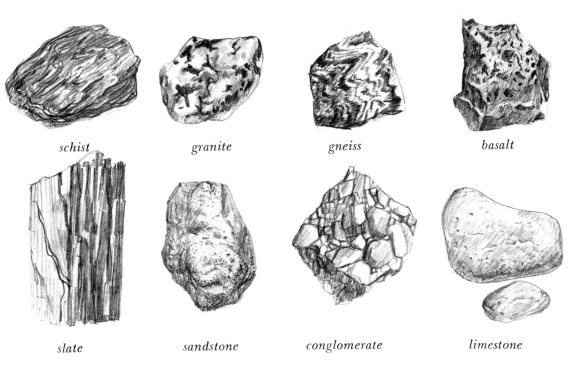

schist   granite   gneiss   basalt

slate   sandstone   conglomerate   limestone

hard and tough to break. It is often used in buildings. It may be pink, red, gray, or brown.

Gneiss (pronounced *nice*) is a large-grained, banded rock. A band of dark-colored minerals is followed by a band of light-colored minerals and so on.

Basalt is a fine-grained, dark-colored rock. It may be black, gray, dark green, or brown. Basalt is a hard rock often used for road building and other construction.

Slate is the rock from which school blackboards are made. It is a hard rock that can easily be split into thin flat sheets.

Sandstone is made up of naturally cemented bits of sand. You can feel the grains of sand when you rub the rock against your hand.

Conglomerate consists of rounded pebbles and gravel, cemented together by nature. It is found mostly in the New England states.

Limestone is made up of particles too small to make out with-

13

out a microscope. This rock is too soft to scratch glass. A drop of vinegar will fizz on limestone. It is usually white, gray, or tan, and is used in making cement. It is also used by farmers to improve soil.

One way to make some kind of order of the many different kinds of rocks is to put them into groups. By grouping things, scientists sort out those that are alike from those that are not alike.

Scientists group rocks together according to the way they were formed. All rocks are formed in one of three ways. *Igneous* rocks form when hot melted rock from inside the earth cools and becomes solid. *Sedimentary* rocks form when clay, sand, and other materials settle out of water and harden. *Metamorphic* rocks form from other kinds of rocks that are changed by pressure and heat.

Of the rocks mentioned above, granite and basalt are igneous. Conglomerate, sandstone, and limestone are sedimentary rocks. Schist, gneiss, and slate are metamorphic rocks.

Look at "Books for Reading and Research" on page 61 for a list of other books that will help you to identify rocks.

You might like to make a collection of the different rocks you find in your vacant lot. You can use an egg carton to keep each group separate. Number each space and write the number and the name of the rock on the lid of the carton. You may be surprised to see how many different kinds of rocks you can find in a vacant lot.

Insects
and Other
Creeping Crawlers

Turn over a large flat rock and look beneath it. You probably will find a number of crawling, creeping, and wiggling animals. Beneath your feet in the soil of a vacant lot live many different kinds of insects, spiders, centipedes, millipedes, snails, earthworms, pill bugs, mites, and many other living things too small to see without a microscope.

Look for these animals beneath rocks, old logs, and pieces of rotting wood. Put your eyes close to the ground and look for ants and spiders making their way through the tangled plants. Listen for the sounds of insects on a hot summer day.

Spread out several sheets of newspaper on the ground. With a shovel, dig up a square foot of soil to a depth of six inches. Spread the soil out on the newspapers. Look for movement in the soil. Count the number of different animals you find. You may be surprised to find out how many there are.

You might like to take home some of the soil and place it in a wide-mouthed glass jar or a small aquarium. Keep the soil moist but not soggy. Cover the top of the jar loosely, so some air can get

in. Observe the soil daily for signs of animal life that you did not notice before.

Of all the different kinds of animals in the world, the largest group by far is insects. About 80 per cent of the different kinds of animals are insects. There are roughly three quarters of a million different kinds of insects known today, and thousands of new ones are discovered each year. They don't all come from strange, distant places either. In New York City, for example, over 15,000 different kinds of insects have been found.

You probably know many kinds of insects, such as ants, flies, termites, cockroaches, butterflies, moths, and beetles. But how can you tell whether a new small creeping animal that you spot is an insect?

Scientists group together animals which are alike in important ways. They don't do it just by how many legs an animal has, or how it moves. They want to know as much as they can about the animal, both inside and outside. Then they decide which ones are most alike in body makeup and in the way their bodies work.

With so many different kinds of insects you can expect to find many differences among them. But all insects are alike in certain important ways. The body of an adult insect is divided into three parts: the *head,* containing the eyes, antennae, and mouth parts; the *thorax,* which has three pairs of jointed legs and often one or two pairs of wings; and the *stomach* or *abdomen,* which contains organs of digestion and reproduction.

Insects go through different stages in their lives, during which their body shape changes. Insects that are not yet adult may look quite different than they will in later life.

Most insects go through four different stages. First there is the egg. Eggs are small and not easily noticed. They come in many

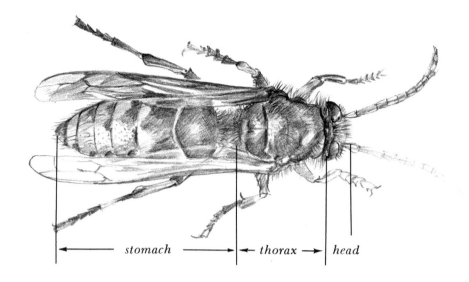

stomach ─────────→ ◄─ thorax ─→ │ head

different colors and shapes. Often they are clumped together. Sometimes they are left on leaves or twigs or in the soil. If you find a cluster of tiny rounded objects, they may be insect eggs. Take them home in a small jar. Keep the jar loosely covered. Observe the objects each day to see if anything hatches.

An insect egg hatches into a wormlike form called a larva. Caterpillars and the "worms" in apples are examples of larvae. You can often find larvae eating the leaves of plants. In fact larvae eat and eat and eat. In a few weeks they usually grow large and fat.

You can collect a caterpillar and observe it in your home. Put

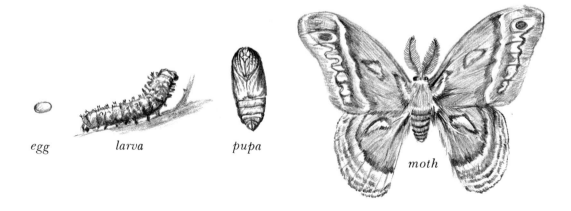

egg   larva   pupa   moth

it in a glass jar along with some of the plant material you find it feeding on. Use an old nylon stocking to cover the top so that the caterpillar cannot escape but air can enter. Every few days put in some fresh plants for the caterpillar to eat.

After a while the caterpillar will stop eating. It will begin to spin a cocoon around itself. Inside the cocoon its body shape changes, and it becomes a pupa. Some insects become pupae without spinning cocoons. Within the pupa great body changes are going on. The pupa is usually motionless and does not eat.

The adult insect emerges from the pupa. With some insects the pupa changes into an adult in a few days. In other insects the change takes a few weeks or even all winter long. You can collect different kinds of cocoons and keep them until they hatch. Most cocoons are drab-looking and difficult to spot. Look for cocoon cases on twigs, leaves, and bushes.

Adult insects are easier to find. Here are some that you will probably see in a vacant lot.

Beetles are very common. There are more kinds of beetles than any other insect. In fact there are more different beetles than all the kinds of mammals, birds, fish, reptiles, and amphibians put together.

The front pair of a beetle's wings are hardened into shields that fold over its body. You may find ladybird beetles, leaf beetles feeding on plants, longicorn beetles with their long antennae, and wood-boring beetles.

Butterflies and moths have two pairs of wings covered with tiny scales. Usually a moth has a fatter body than a butterfly and comes out in the evening, while a butterfly is about during the day. A moth's antennae are often feathery, while a butterfly's antennae are usually thin.

Ants, wasps, and bees usually live in large groups called colonies. These three are the only insects with stingers—so don't grab for a bee or a wasp with your hands. An ant's stinger is not usually so dangerous. Look for ant nests under large rocks or in rotting wood.

Flies come in different sizes and colors. They all have large eyes and small antennae.

Other insects that you may find on a lot include grasshoppers, mantises, crickets, termites, aphids, cockroaches, and lacewings.

You can keep some of these adult insects as pets. A praying mantis makes an interesting pet. Place one in a glass jar along with some twigs. Cover the jar with something so that the mantis cannot escape but air can pass through. Feed your mantis small live insects. Watch how it uses its front legs to grasp the insect. From time to time sprinkle a few drops of water in the jar.

Ants may be even more interesting to keep and watch. You will need a large wide-mouthed glass jar and its cover. Find an ant nest in a piece of rotting wood or in the ground. Quickly collect plenty of ants, ant cocoons, eggs, and some of the wood or the soil. Place them in the jar and cover them. Some of the ants will probably run out of the jar, but just keep collecting. If you find a very large ant, take it. It may be a queen.

At home, cover the sides of the jar with black paper. Place the jar in a flat pan half-filled with water to prevent the ants from escaping. Remove the jar's cover. Sprinkle a few drops of water on a piece of sponge and place it in the jar. Feed the ants on a bit of potato, bread crumbs, a drop of jam or jelly, and a dead soft-bodied insect or piece of worm.

Remove the black paper when you want to observe the ants. You will see them tunneling in the soil and caring for the eggs

20

and cocoons. Your ants may live for many weeks, but without a
queen the colony will die after a while.

Not every small crawly animal is an insect. Spiders are not insects; they belong to a class of animals called *Arachnida*. They
have two body parts and four pairs of legs, rather than an insect's
three body parts and three pairs of legs. Spiders also differ from
insects in having several (up to eight) simple eyes. Insects have a
pair of many-sided compound eyes.

Spiders eat insects and are very helpful to man because of this.
They have fangs which are used to inject poison into their larger
prey. Most spiders cannot hurt you in any way. One exception is
the black widow spider. You probably won't come across a black
widow; but if you do, you can recognize it by its deep black color
and a bright red hourglass marking on its underside. It is about a
half-inch long.

You can find a spider most easily by looking for its web. Look
for webs on bushes or in grass. Spiders make their webs from silk,
which they spin from a liquid made in their bodies. The silk

threads come out of a set of openings in the spider's abdomen. The silk can come out in different ways—as flat bands, fine strands, or thick cables.

Spiders use silk not only to make webs but to make sacs for their eggs, as anchor lines, and as parachutes or balloons. A young spider launches itself into the air at the end of a long silk thread. You can sometimes feel a spider's silk thread when you accidentally brush against it.

Most spiders trap the insects they eat in their webs. But some spiders hunt their prey without spinning webs. You may find these wolf spiders and jumping spiders in the undergrowth of the lot. Jumping spiders are active in daylight and are often brightly colored. Wolf spiders are drabber looking and hunt at night. A daddy longlegs, by the way, is not really a spider at all. It belongs to a closely related group of jointed-leg animals whose bodies appear to be one solid part.

The bodies of centipedes and millipedes are made up of many parts or segments. Centipedes have one pair of legs for each segment, while millipedes have two pairs of legs for each segment. Centipedes prey on insects and have poison fangs formed from the first pair of legs. A large centipede can give you a nasty bite, so handle it carefully. Millipedes eat only plant material and are slow moving. It's fun to watch either of these animals move. Sometimes their many legs seem to trip over one another.

Snails, slugs, earthworms, pill bugs, and other kinds of small animals can often be found under heaps of rotting plants or decaying wood. You have only to look around.

Weeds,
Seeds,
and Flowers

Weeds are plants that people often don't like to see growing. Weeds may grow in places where only certain other plants are wanted. Farmers, for example, try to get rid of weeds growing among their crops. Weeds are harmful to man in a few cases. Poison ivy, which irritates the skin, and ragweed, which is bad for hay-fever sufferers, are examples of harmful plants.

Vacant lots are usually full of different kinds of plants. Almost every bit of soil has something growing in it. Most people call these plants weeds. But to a scientist these plants are interesting to study and find out about. One person's weed is another person's plant.

Many weeds are tough, hardy plants. They grow just about anywhere. You'll find weeds growing in the cracks of sidewalks, in small pockets of soil atop rocks, and almost anywhere they can get through to the ground.

Some weeds are very pretty too. Gardeners call the dandelion a pest because new ones keep coming up where they're not wanted. But in a vacant lot, where no one cares which plants grow, you can appreciate their beauty.

You can recognize a dandelion by its yellow flowers set in a circlet of toothed leaves. Look for it in the spring. Pick a dandelion flower and you'll find that it is set on a hollow stalk. The stems and leaves hold a milky juice called latex. Milkweed is another plant that contains latex. Try uprooting a dandelion. The root is long and difficult to pull up. Now you know one reason why dandelions are so hard to get rid of.

When a dandelion has a white mane, its seeds are mature. Blow on one and watch the seeds as they are carried off by the wind. It might be fun to try to count the number of seeds on a single dandelion. Each seed could become a new dandelion if it lands in a place where it can grow. It's not difficult to see why dandelions are so common.

Other kinds of plants that may grow in a vacant lot are great ragweed, common ragweed, common yarrow, plantain, buckhorn, chickweed, quackgrass, lamb's-quarters, and crabgrass. All of these are flowering plants, but on some the flowers are tiny and hard to see. For example, in the spring, chickweed has many little white flowers about one-sixteenth of an inch across. If you look carefully, you'll see that even short grasses have tiny flowers.

Find a large flower and look at it closely. Use a magnifying glass if you have one. In the center of the flower are its reproductive parts. One part, called the stamen, has a fuzzy top. The top contains tiny grains of a yellowish powder called *pollen*. The thin tubes in the middle of the flower are called *pistils*.

Pollen is blown by the wind or carried by insects from the stamen of one flower to the pistil of the same or another flower. The pollen grain produces a hollow tube which grows down into the pistil. A part of the pollen grain, called the *sperm cell*, goes through the tube and unites with a cell called an *ovule*. Scien-

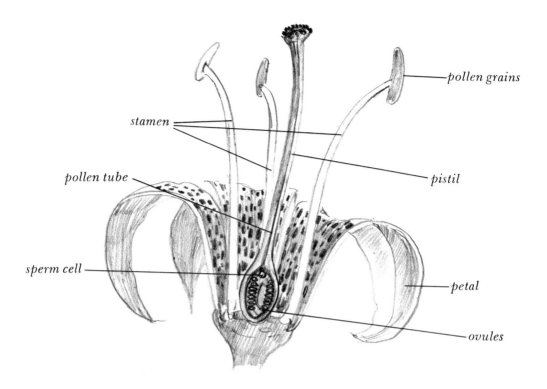

pollen grains

stamen

pollen tube

sperm cell

pistil

petal

ovules

tists say that the ovule has then been fertilized. A fertilized ovule becomes a seed. Every single plant seed came from a flower in a similar way.

Make a collection of all the different kinds of seeds you find in the lot. You may find winged maple seeds, acorns from oaks, burs that stick to your clothing, seeds from plants of all kinds.

Some of the seeds are spread by the wind; others stick to the coats of animals or to clothing and may be accidentally carried to distant places. Still other seeds are eaten by animals because they are contained in the fruit of the plant. These seeds, such as those in berries, then come out in animal droppings. Seeds are also spread by streams and rivers and even by being shot out by some plants. When ripe, the jewelweed or touch-me-not shoots out its seeds several feet if barely touched.

Almost every patch of soil has some seeds in it. Collect some soil in a clean can or a milk container with its top removed. Take the soil home and sprinkle some water on it. Keep the soil moist but not muddy. After a few days or a week you'll probably find some seedlings growing in the soil. The seedlings sprouted from seeds hidden in the soil.

Not all plants flower and produce seeds. Nonflowering plants include lichens, mosses, ferns, and mushrooms. Lichens often form a greenish-gray crust on rocks or tree trunks. Mosses are low-growing plants that form a green carpet in wet weather but look brown and dead in dry weather. A good rainfall turns them green again. Ferns have thin branching stems and small leaves. They need a good deal of moisture. Mushrooms and other re-lated plants grow on dead and decaying plant material. They, too, need much moisture.

Plants protect themselves from harm in different ways. Some plants have thorns or spines on them. These cut and hurt animals that may come near. Look at the plants in a vacant lot and pick out those that have thorns. Do people and animals harm these plants as much as plants without this protection? Of course, thorns don't protect against insects.

SOME KINDS OF SEEDS WHICH MAY BE FOUND IN A VACANT LOT

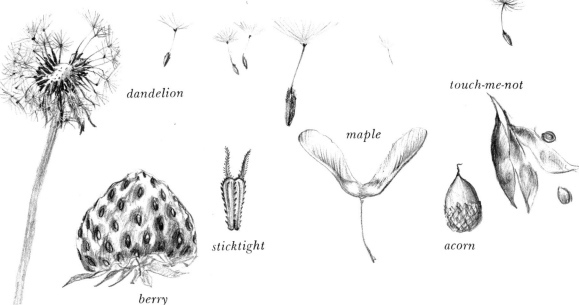

dandelion

touch-me-not

maple

sticktight

acorn

berry

thistle *poison ivy* *skunk cabbage*

THREE PLANTS WITH SPECIAL WAYS OF PROTECTING THEMSELVES

Some plants are protected from being touched because they are poisonous in one way or another. For example, contact with the oily sap in the roots, stems, or leaves of poison ivy often causes an itchy rash and blisters.

Poison ivy is a three-leafed vine or thin shrub. The upper surfaces of the leaves are shiny, and they are usually deeply notched. The leaves are green in spring and summer but turn a dark red in the fall. Small white berries also appear in the fall.

If you find posion ivy growing in the lot, stay away from it. Even if the oily sap just gets on your clothing, it may give you a rash if you touch it later. Burning the poison ivy isn't much help. The poisonous oil gets in the smoke and is still dangerous.

Plants are protected in other ways too. Some plants, such as the skunk cabbage, have bad odors. Others, such as milkweed,

28

have bad tastes. Some, such as certain kinds of mushrooms, are poisonous to eat. Many plants have tough woody stems that make eating them difficult.

There are many things you can do to find out about the plants in a vacant lot. Here are some that you might like to try.

Do plant leaves need air to live? You will need some Vaseline to find out. Find a plant in the lot in an out-of-the-way spot. Cover four of the leaves on the plant on both sides with Vaseline. In two or three days wipe the Vaseline from two of the leaves. Compare the color of the two leaves with that of the leaves that were not covered with Vaseline. Which are greener? Keep the other two leaves covered with Vaseline. After a few days they will turn yellow and fall off. Can you explain why?

Do plant leaves need sunlight? Find out with some black paper and a few paper clips. Clip a piece of paper on each side of four leaves. In a few days remove the paper from two of the leaves and compare their color with uncovered leaves. What happens to the leaves that remain covered a few days longer? How do you explain this?

You can show that plant leaves give off water into the air. You will need a plastic bag and a piece of string. Place the plastic bag over some of the leaves and tie the bottom of the bag closed. In a few hours the plastic bag will have a film of water covering the inside. To make sure that it is the leaves that give off water, tie the plastic bag around a twig or other plant part without leaves. See if water forms inside the plastic bag this time.

Can some plants get too much water? Try watering heavily one small plant in the lot every day. Each day compare it with another similar plant. What effect does the watering have? Would the same results be true of all plants?

Do some sections of the lot get more sun during the day than other sections? Do the same kinds of plants grow in both sunny and shady parts of the lot? If there is a tree growing in the lot, look at the plants growing in its shade. Are these plants the same kinds as those in other shady spots?

Make a collection of different leaves. At home lay the leaves flat between a few sheets of newspaper. Press them down with several books until they dry. If you like, you can wax each leaf by putting it between pieces of waxed paper and pressing it with a warm iron. The dried or waxed leaves can be mounted on cards and labeled. You can use some of the books listed on pages 61-62 or other books in your library to find out the names of the leaves.

Trees

Many vacant lots have at least one tree growing in them. Even if your vacant lot has no trees, you can probably find one planted along a street. Look for trees around your neighborhood or in front of your school. Even in the middle of a crowded city there are trees. New York City, for example, has over one million trees planted along its streets.

Plan to visit a nearby tree regularly. You can watch how the tree changes with the seasons, the different animals that visit it, and how it affects the area around it.

Look over your tree carefully. Have a friend stand next to it and try to guess the tree's height. Is it three times as tall as your friend, six times as tall, ten times as tall? Look at the way the branches are attached to the trunk. Do they come in straight or at a slant? Feel the bark. Is it rough or smooth? What color is it?

Look at one of the leaves. Does one leaf grow on each stem or is there more than one? Does the leaf have toothed edges or is it smooth? What is its shape? Can you see any flowers, fruits, or seeds? Learning these things about your tree will help to identify it.

Here are some kinds of trees that are often planted along city streets. Some trees are found in just one section of the country; other kinds may be found planted in cities all over the country.

A pin oak's bottom branches slant downward. Its leaf has five to seven deeply cut edges. Like all kinds of oaks, a pin oak has acorns. A pin oak's acorns are small and rounded. Its leaves turn dark red in the fall.

A Norway maple has a broad leaf, as wide as it is long. Just before the leaves open in spring, the tree is covered with clusters of yellowish-green flowers. The yellow pollen from the flowers often covers the ground beneath the tree. The seeds which develop from the flowers are double-winged.

A London plane tree is most easily recognized by its two-colored trunk, which looks as if it's peeling. The London plane is related to the American sycamore tree, and you may find either planted along the streets. The seed clusters are in a spiked ball called a *buttonball*. American sycamores usually have one buttonball on a stalk; London plane trees usually have two.

Locust trees are tall thin trees encircled by thorns. They have many small rounded leaflets on each stalk. Black Locusts have clusters of white flowers in the spring. Honey locusts have greenish flowers.

Tulip trees are so called because of their greenish-yellow flowers which look something like tulips. The bark of a tulip tree is thick and heavily ridged. Many small winged seeds form upright seed pods on the tree. The leaves begin to turn yellow in late August.

A ginkgo or maidenhair tree has leaves like little wavy-edged fans with a wedge cut out. Ginkgo trees are rather odd. They come in two kinds: male and female. Only the female tree bears

pin oak

Norway maple

London plane tree

fruit. The ginkgo tree is the oldest kind of tree known. Ginkgo trees very much like the ones you see growing in cities today lived more than one hundred million years ago in the time of the dinosaurs.

An ailanthus tree will grow almost anywhere in the city. It grows on the smallest patch of hard soil. You might think of it as a weed tree. Its other name is tree of heaven, but maybe a better name would be stink tree. Crush some of the leaflets together and you'll see why. The odor is awful. You can recognize an ailanthus by its long fernlike leaves, each with fifteen to thirty leaflets. It bears two kinds of flowers, one of which also has a bad odor.

Many other trees grow wild on vacant lots. You may find oaks, maples, wild cherries, beeches, birches, and others. One of the books listed on pages 61-62 will help you to identify these trees.

Look at the place where the tree is growing. Trees grow toward the light. If a tall building is set on one side of a tree, the branches on the other side may be much larger.

34

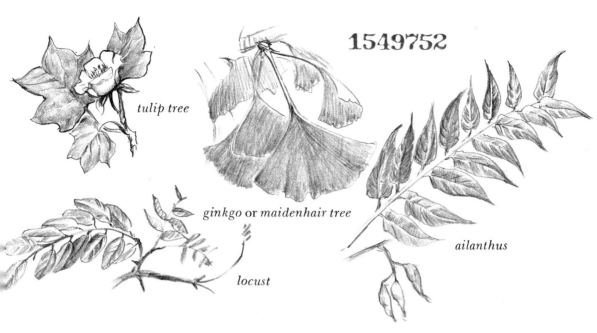

tulip tree

ginkgo or maidenhair tree

ailanthus

locust

Trees that grow in a city have to overcome smoke, dust, and all sorts of other unfavorable conditions. Examine the bark of the tree. Has it been injured by people cutting it? Do you see scars where branches may have been cut off? Have animals such as dogs and cats injured the bark? Bark protects the tree. It grows over cuts and covers them. If the bark is stripped from a tree, it will die.

You may see where a branch has been cut from a tree and a ring of bark has grown back around it. Look for broken branches on the tree. These are often spots where insects and diseases enter the wood of the tree and cause it to rot. Sometimes the rotten wood of a tree is carved away by man, and a special cement is put in the hole. This helps to protect the tree from further rotting.

The leaves of a tree will tell you much about its condition. Drooping or curling leaves may mean that the tree is not getting enough water. The tree may not get enough water even when it rains. The water must go into the ground and reach the tree's roots. If the soil around the tree is hard and tightly packed, the water just runs off without going into the ground. You can help

35

such a tree get enough water by breaking up the top two inches of the soil.

A tree may have as large a root system under the soil as it has branches above the ground. The large root system is needed because a tree takes in so much water. Even a small tree needs many gallons of water each week. When the tree is getting enough water and the minerals it needs, its leaves are green and healthy-looking.

Look for large and small animals that use the tree and depend upon it. By late summer you will rarely find a single leaf on the trees that doesn't have an insect hole in it. You may find insects eating at leaves or in the cracks in the bark of the tree. Look also for spider webs strung from the branches of the tree. Can you tell how spiders help the tree?

Larger animals may also be found in the tree. Squirrels often leap from branch to branch in larger trees. Perhaps you will see them gathering acorns or other seeds. In the winter you may see a clump of dried leaves high in the branches of the tree. This is probably a squirrel nest.

You'll often see birds using a tree. They may be sitting on a branch preening their feathers with their bills or searching the tree for insects or seeds to eat. You may even see a bird building a nest. Be sure you don't disturb the nest, for any eggs or young birds in it may die.

A tree makes different weather conditions for the living things around it. Stand under a tree on a hot day. It is much cooler there and not nearly as bright as in an unprotected spot. Trees break the force of the wind and the falling rain. They bind the soil with their roots and keep it from being washed away. Trees provide shelter and food for many different animals.

Bird
Visitors

Look for signs of bird life in a vacant lot. You may find feathers on the ground, an abandoned nest in a tree, or bird tracks on the ground. You may hear the sounds of birds in the air. Look for birds hopping or running along the ground, moving through the bushes and the grass, or sitting on a tree branch. It won't take you long to spot a bird somewhere.

One city bird that you're almost sure to find visiting the lot from time to time is the pigeon. Pigeons nest on the ledges of buildings and other high places, but they search everywhere for food. Food for a pigeon is just about anything: seeds, insects, earthworms, scraps of meat or fish, whatever is around.

Pigeons are large chunky birds. They are usually gray or blue, but you may see other colors as well. Their feet are red, and their bills are black. Look for their three-toed tracks in snow or mud.

Pigeons have remarkable eyesight. They will feed on a crowded street among rushing cars, trucks, and people and just avoid getting hit at the last moment. If you feed them bits of a cracker or a piece of bread, they will spot every last crumb.

pigeons

Pigeons are not as afraid of people as many other birds. You may see someone feeding pigeons out of his hand. But this trust only goes so far. If you've ever run after a pigeon, you know that you just can't catch it.

Pigeons lay two to four eggs almost any season of the year. They may raise more than one brood each year. In New York City alone some scientists think that there are a quarter of a million pigeons. Pigeons have multiplied and spread since migrating to the United States with the early colonists. They originally came as domestic animals, but many became wild.

You'll most often see pigeons traveling together in flocks. The size of the flock seems to depend on the amount of food available. If a single pigeon finds some food, it won't be long before he is joined by other birds in the flock.

Another city bird that travels in flocks is the starling. A starling is smaller in size than a pigeon; it may travel in even larger flocks. A mature starling is shiny black with white spots on its back. Its bill is yellow in summer and darker in winter. A young starling is as large as an adult bird but is gray and spotted with white.

Starlings were imported into the United States from Europe in 1890. Sixty and then forty more starlings were released in Central Park in New York City. From this small band of one hundred birds have come the millions of starlings now found all over the country.

Many large flocks of starlings live in the heart of big cities. Each morning they scatter to the outskirts of the city in a search for food. It is these large central flocks of starlings that have given the bird a bad name in some places. In one place the birds gathered in such numbers on the hands of the city clock that they stopped it from moving.

starling

The third city bird you're liable to see is the English sparrow or house sparrow. Like the pigeon and the starling, the house sparrow was also introduced into the United States. It was released in Brooklyn, New York, in 1850. By 1900 the sparrow was the most common bird in the cities. But since automobiles took the place of the horse in transportation, sparrows are not as numerous as they once were. Horses eat oats and other grains. As horses disappeared there was less grain for the sparrows to feed upon. This resulted in fewer sparrows. But they have found other sources of food and are still around in good numbers.

The sparrow is a smaller bird than either the pigeon or the starling. It has a brown back and white and black underparts. Sparrows travel in small flocks. When they land in a vacant lot, you'll see them hopping around and chirping as they search for food. Besides grain, sparrows eat seeds, fruit, insects, and scraps of food from garbage.

Sparrows nest almost anywhere: fire escapes, ledges, holes in trees, and buildings of all kinds. Three to six grayish-white eggs speckled with dark green are laid in the nest. Young birds soon begin to travel with the flock and are fed by all the adults in the flock, not just the parents.

sparrows

red-winged blackbird

wren

woodpecker

catbird

robin

crow

blue jay

You may see other birds from time to time in a vacant lot. Look for robins searching for worms and other insects. Blue jays are large birds with a crest atop their heads. Crows, wrens, blackbirds, chickadees, catbirds, and woodpeckers are other possible visitors.

Spring and fall are the best times of the year in most parts of the country to look for birds. During these seasons many birds are passing through on their migrations to the north or to the south. But even during the winter there are birds about. In fact you'll always see more different kinds of birds in a vacant lot than any other larger animals.

All birds have feathers, two wings, and two legs. They all lay eggs and are warm-blooded. But beyond this birds differ from one kind to another. You can learn much about these differences by careful observation.

Here are some of the things to look for. How large is the bird? Compare it to another bird such as a robin or a sparrow. Is the bird alone or in a pair or in a flock? What is its shape and color? Does it have special markings on its body such as stripes or spots? Does it fly in a straight line or move up and down? Does it hop or run on the ground or perch on the side of a tree? What kind of food does it seems to eat? What shape and color is its bill? What kind of sounds does it make?

These observations will tell you about the bird's habits and will also help you identify it. Make notes about your observations and then check one of the books about bird identification listed on pages 61-62. Don't be discouraged if at first you can't tell which bird is which. Keep watching and making notes, and you will soon be able to tell one kind from another.

Birds are one of the few kinds of larger wild animals that you can observe every day in a vacant lot. Here, even in the midst of a city, they will go about their daily activities just as if no one were there to watch. Birds bring nature a little closer to city dwellers.

Animal
Visitors

From time to time you may see dogs, cats, squirrels, and rats and mice in a vacant lot. Perhaps you may even find someone's escaped pet, such as a turtle, a hamster, or a snake. Look for holes or burrows in the ground that these animals might use.

Dogs and men have lived closely together for a long time, perhaps ten thousand years or more. Dogs helped man in many ways. They guarded his home and family. They helped to protect his herds. They hunted with him. They became his friends.

Nowadays dogs that live with people in a city don't have all these jobs to do. Many dogs bark at strangers and will protect their masters, but most dogs today are kept just because of the friendship they offer to man.

The dogs that you see in a vacant lot usually come with their masters. Watch how they act. They run around sniffing, tails wagging, scratching, barking, and so on. Perhaps you may see a dog bury some food in the ground.

If the dog comes near you, don't make sudden movements. Talk softly to it and let it smell your fingers. Ask the dog's master

if you may pet it. Don't try doing any of these things with a stray dog. A stray may be unfriendly to people and can be dangerous.

Dogs find out many things by using their noses. Watch how a dog sniffs at something to identify it. The master allows a dog to smell a stick and then throws it away. If the dog doesn't see where the stick lands, it may locate it by its odor. A dog can often tell an article of its master's clothing by the way it smells. Dogs seem to enjoy running around a vacant lot. You can enjoy watching what they do.

Cats have also lived with man for a long time. But while dogs seem to have lost much of their wild past, cats become wild more easily. You won't find too many stray dogs around, but almost every neighborhood has lots of stray cats.

Watch how a cat walks through the grass in a vacant lot. It looks like a miniature tiger. See how it stalks its prey—a mouse or a large insect. The cat creeps up quietly, one foot at a time. Its eyes stare unblinkingly at its victim. Its tail twitches back and forth. Suddenly it pounces, claws extended.

Cats can take care of themselves in the city. When they become wild, they don't need man and will have nothing to do with him. It is a good idea to have nothing to do with such cats. They won't hesitate to scratch or bite.

Many of the stray cats in a city live by hunting rats and mice. Stray cats mate, have kittens, and often the kittens become strays too.

Without cats, rats and mice would be even more of a serious problem than they are now. You may not see a rat or a mouse in a vacant lot; but whether you see them or not, they are there.

Rats are nighttime animals. When darkness falls, rats come out of their holes from inside the walls of houses, from the sewers, from garbage piles, from dark underground places all over.

Most of the rats in a city are Norway rats. They also have other names such as sewer rats, brown rats, and house rats. A Norway rat weighs about one pound, and its body is from eight to eighteen inches long. Its naked, scaly tail is shorter than its body, about six inches long. The fur is usually matted and grayish- or reddish-brown.

Rats breed very quickly and in great numbers. A rat may have six litters a year, usually with eight to twelve in each litter. The young are born blind and without fur, but their helpless state doesn't last for long. After one month they are out on their own. After three or four months they can mate and produce young. One scientist figured out that one pair of rats could multiply to *one hundred billion* in a little over five years if conditions were right. Of course, things are never that good for rats. Disease, shortage of food, and enemies such as cats and man all take their toll.

But the rats that do live are bad enough. Rats eat and spoil millions of dollars worth of food each year. A rat's teeth grow several inches each year. To prevent its teeth from becoming too long, the rat must constantly gnaw at hard objects. Rats gnaw through cardboard boxes, walls, even tin cans and lead pipes.

Norway rat   *house mouse*

They eat almost anything and will gnaw through almost anything to get at food.

Not only do rats eat our valuable food, but they also carry diseases. Either by carrying germs on their bodies or by way of the lice and fleas that live on them, rats have spread typhus, plague, rabies, and other diseases, including rat-bite fever. A cornered rat will turn and bite a man; they also bite infants and other helpless people.

Man fights against rats by using special kinds of poison. New concrete buildings are ratproof. But the best way to control rats is by seeing that they have as little food as possible. This means putting garbage in pails and keeping the lids on tight. It means getting rid of rubbish so that rats cannot live there. It means putting food in containers and not leaving it out in the open. These things may not get rid of rats completely, but they will help.

Mice are another kind of animal that lives around man. You are more likely to see a mouse in a vacant lot than a rat. Mice are smaller than rats. The common house mouse is about four inches long and has a three-inch tail. Its color is brownish-gray to light

47

black. It roams around mostly at night, but you may see it going from one place to another during the day.

Mice breed almost as quickly as rats. A mouse is able to breed at two months of age. Within one year a single pair of mice can multiply to over one thousand.

Mice are not as vicious as rats. They don't often bite people. But they are a serious nuisance anyway. They damage food and clothing. They carry many kinds of disease. One kind of house mouse is helpful to man, however. That is a special strain of white mouse used in many scientific experiments.

Squirrels are related to rats and mice but are much nicer animals as far as man is concerned. Squirrels live in trees, eat acorns and seeds of all kinds, and are lively, interesting animals to watch.

Gray squirrels are the kind you're likely to see in a vacant lot. Watch them chattering away, chasing each other up and down trees, and nibbling at nuts. Squirrels in the city often become friendly enough to eat peanuts or bread crumbs out of people's hands. This is not a good idea, however, because a squirrel can accidentally give you a nasty bite.

Squirrels sometimes eat food that is put out for birds. For this reason a bird feeder often has a shield or guard built on it to prevent squirrels from getting at the food. The guard is not usually successful, though. Squirrels are very acrobatic and can get around most guards.

Squirrels nest in holes in trees or make nests out of leaves on a high branch. You can see their nests easily in the fall and winter, when the trees are bare. Young squirrels are often born in the summer. When they are six weeks old, they leave the nest and begin to look for food themselves.

Exploring
All Year Long

Exploring in a vacant lot is an all-year-round activity. There is much to see in spring, summer, fall, even in winter. Here's a roundup of things to do during each season.

In the Spring

Look at the buds on trees and bushes. Many will be swelling or opening. See how the leaves are folded into the bud. On which kinds of trees do the leaves come out earliest? Does the weather have anything to do with the time the trees leaf? What happens to leaves on a cold spring day?

Look for dandelions and other early season flowers. See if bees and other insects are attracted to them. Watch how the insect burrows into the flower. It is getting the sweet nectar to eat. But in going after the nectar the insect also picks up some pollen. When it travels to another flower, some of the pollen drops off. In this way the ovules of a plant are fertilized by the pollen of another plant. When ovules are fertilized, a fruit develops around them. Without insect pollination many kinds of fruit, such as apples and cherries, would not develop.

49

Look at bare patches of soil in the lot. See if any new seedlings are beginning to show. Bare patches of soil are soon used by one kind of plant or another. By late spring there will be few bare spots left.

Birds are migrating northward now. Look for unfamiliar kinds in the trees and bushes. Perhaps you may see some stop off to hunt for insects or other food. Remember to note some things about them so that you can identify them later in a field guide.

Squirrels look shabby in the spring. They are losing parts of their thick winter fur. During very cold and severe winters squirrels may go into a long winter sleep called *hibernation*. But during more mild winters squirrels are up and about often. If the winter has been severe, look to see if the squirrels seem thin.

In the Summer

Summertime is insect time. Look and listen for insects in the lot. Perhaps you will hear a cricket in the early evening. Crickets chirp faster when the temperature is higher. In fact there is a formula for finding the temperature by counting the number of cricket chirps in fifteen seconds and adding forty. Try out the formula on both warm and cool nights to see if it works.

Examine some of the plants growing in the lot. Can you tell which of the plants belongs to the family of grass? The grass family is a very large one. It includes such tall grasses as bamboo, sugarcane, corn, wheat, and rice, as well as the more familiar lawn grasses.

Here's how to recognize a member of the grass family. All grasses have a stem with solid joints. At each joint a leaf grows in an opposite direction from the one above and the one below. The leaf is longer than it is wide, and part of it is always wrapped around the stem.

Find a sawed-off branch or an old tree trunk. The rings tell you how old that branch or that tree is. Each ring represents a growth season of one year. Count the rings. The number is the same as the age in years.

A wide ring shows a good year of growth for the tree. There must have been lots of rain and enough sunshine during the growing season. A narrow ring shows the reverse: not enough rain and a poor growing season.

Watch for sparrows and other birds bathing themselves in puddles of water after a rain. During dry periods birds dust them-

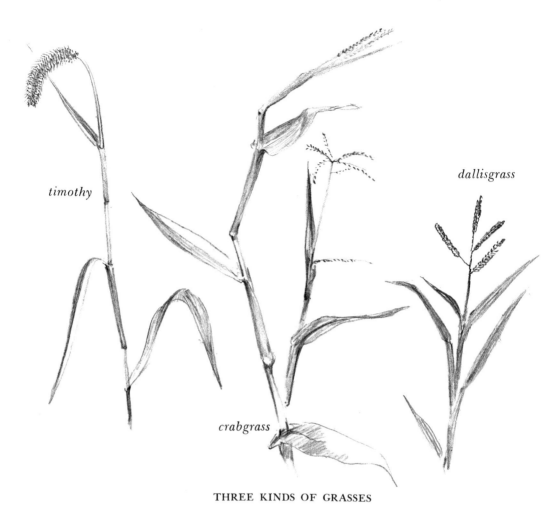

timothy

dallisgrass

crabgrass

THREE KINDS OF GRASSES

selves with dry loose soil. They flutter in the dust just as they do in the water. This probably helps them get rid of insect pests in their feathers.

On a hot day feel the temperature of the sidewalk and compare it to the temperature of a grass-covered spot in the lot. Which is hotter? Plants absorb some of the sun's rays and keep the ground cooler than the unprotected sidewalk. Can you tell why the city in summer is usually hotter than the country?

Look for little mounds of earth on top of the soil. These are earthworm casts. Earthworms tunnel through the soil eating plant material. The casts are the remains of an earthworm's meal. Earthworms help to mix the soil and make it better for plants.

In the Fall

Make a collection of autumn leaves. The leaves of each kind of tree turn a certain color. See if you can identify the color of oak leaves and maple leaves. Warm days and cool nights are needed for a good leaf display in the fall. Note which trees lose their leaves earliest, which latest.

Look at the leaf scar left on a twig. Before a leaf falls, a layer of corklike material forms beneath the stem. This allows the leaf to fall off and at the same time seals the place from which the leaf grew. Trees that lose their leaves in the fall are called *deciduous*.

Those that keep their leaves in winter are called *evergreens*. The evergreens that bear cones, such as pine, spruce, and fir trees, are used for Christmas trees.

Look for insect eggs and cocoons on bushes and beneath rocks and logs. Eggs are all different shapes. It is difficult to tell what

COCOONS

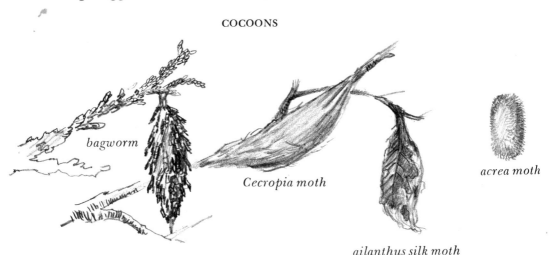

bagworm

Cecropia moth

acrea moth

ailanthus silk moth

kind of an insect will hatch from the eggs that you find. Some of them may be from a spider, slug, or other small animal.

Collect seeds of different kinds from bushes, grasses, and trees. Many of the seeds will be packed together in some way. Open one of these seed packages and count the number of seeds within. Do you think that most of these seeds will grow into plants? Could all the seeds on all the plants grow into new plants? Why not? Can you tell how the seeds are spread: by animals, wind, or just dropping?

Look at the buds on trees and bushes. How are they protected against the winter? Open one of the buds and note the leaves or the flowers folded within. Most buds must go through a long period of cold weather before they will burst into bloom. This prevents them from mistakenly blooming during a short spell of warm fall weather and then dying when winter comes.

Animals get ready for the coming winter in different ways. Look for squirrels gathering and storing acorns and other foods. Look for birds migrating south. You'll often see flocks of migrating birds overhead during the autumn.

In the Winter

Look for birds during the winter. What kind of food do they eat? Many of them depend upon people feeding them. Watch how their feathers fluff out on cold days. The feathers are full of tiny air pockets that act as insulators so that the birds will stay warm. Also look for abandoned bird nests at this time of year. The branches of trees are bare, and you can see the nests more easily.

Don't remove the nests because they may be used by the birds next spring.

Look for tracks of birds and other animals in the snow. Can you tell what kind of an animal made the prints? Note the way the tracks go: in a straight line or stopping and zigzagging. Does this tell you if the animal was looking for food or just walking?

Does one inch of snow make one inch of water? Remove the top of an empty milk container. Fill it full of snow. Take it into a warm place and let the snow melt. How much water is in the container? Different kinds of snow contain different amounts of water. Loose snow has less water than wet, tightly packed snow.

Go out to the lot after a snowstorm. Notice how the trees and bushes are loaded down by the weight of the snow. Have any branches been torn off by the storm? Branches snap more easily when they are frozen than at other times. As the sun comes out and the snow begins to melt, the branches may become covered with sheets of glistening ice.

Under a blanket of snow the ground is warmer than it would be if exposed to the air. If you have an outdoor thermometer, check the ground temperature under the snow and compare it to the air temperature. Also check the temperature beneath a pile of rotting leaves. Leaves and snow are good insulators. They protect the ground below the surface from freezing solid. This helps to prevent animals and plant roots in the soil from freezing solid and dying.

Look at the cracks in rocks or bricks. Water gets into the cracks and then freezes and turns into ice. The ice expands, widening the cracks. Bits of rock may be split off from the main piece in this way.

If the
Bulldozer
Comes

A lot in a city may not remain vacant for long. One day men and machines may come and start to construct a building. Here is a chance for you to observe some new things about the lot.

Builders often use a power shovel to dig deep cuts in the soil. See if you can pick out the darker-colored layer of topsoil from the lighter-colored layer of subsoil. What is in the subsoil: rocks, clay, gravel, sand, or a mixture of these? Is the topsoil heaped in a mound for later use? Topsoil is good for lawn areas or other plantings. What happens to the soil when the plant covering has been stripped away and it rains?

Perhaps there is very little soil before the builder strikes bedrock. Bedrock is part of the earth's crust. It extends down for many miles into the earth. In some places, bedrock is covered by many feet of soil. In other places, bedrock lies just a few feet below the soil or may even be at the surface.

Has the builder uprooted any trees in the lot? Look at the size of the tree's root system. Now you can see why a tree is so difficult to turn over. Roots not only hold a tree firmly in the soil but supply the tree with the water and dissolved minerals it needs.

In some places, digging turns up some interesting objects in the ground. In New York City, for example, excavations sometimes come upon Indian arrowheads or traces of early settlements, such as clay pipes or kitchen utensils. You might also find minerals and fossils. Fossils are the remains of animals or plants of long ago that have been naturally preserved in the earth's crust.

What happens to the animal and plant life in the lot during construction? Some animals just move to a new location. Others may not be able to move and will die. Do any plants remain or will the builder put in new plants afterward?

Man changes nature in many ways. You can look at and think about some of these changes in your no-longer-vacant lot. Then, perhaps, you can find another vacant lot to explore.

Books
for Reading
and Research

Dowden, Ann O. *Look at a Flower*. New York: Thomas Y. Crowell Company, 1963.

Golden Nature Guide Series. New York: Golden Press.
  Cottam, Clarence, and Zim, Herbert S. *Insects*. 1951.
  Gabrielson, Ira N., and Zim, Herbert S. *Birds*. 1949.
  Martin, Alexander C., and Zim, Herbert S. *Trees*. 1952.
  Shaffer, Paul R., and Zim, Herbert S. *Rocks and Minerals,* 1957.

Hogner, D. C. *Weeds*. New York: Thomas Y. Crowell Company, 1968.

Hutchins, Ross E. *The Amazing Seeds*. New York: Dodd, Mead and Company, 1965.

Pearl, Richard M. *How to Know the Minerals and Rocks*. New York: McGraw-Hill Book Company, 1955.

Peterson, Roger T. *A Field Guide to the Birds*. rev. ed. Boston: Houghton Mifflin Company, 1964.

Peterson, Roger T. *How to Know the Birds*. Boston: Houghton Mifflin Company, 1962.

Rogers, Matilda. *A First Book of Tree Identification*. New York: Random House, 1951.

Selsam, Millicent E. *Play with Seeds*. New York: William Morrow and Company, 1957.

Simon, Hilda. *Insect Masquerades*. New York: The Viking Press, 1968.

Simon, Seymour. *Animals in Field and Laboratory: Science Projects in Animal Behavior*. New York: McGraw-Hill Book Company, 1968.

Simon, Seymour. *Discovering What Earthworms Do*. New York: McGraw-Hill Book Company, 1969.

Stefferud, Alfred. *The Wonders of Seeds*. New York: Harcourt, Brace and World, 1956.

Sterling, Dorothy. *Caterpillars*. New York: Doubleday and Company, 1961.

Teale, Edwin W. *Insect Friends*. New York: Dodd, Mead and Company, 1955.

Teale, Edwin W. *The Junior Book of Insects*. rev. ed. New York: E. P. Dutton and Company, 1953.

Youngpeter, John M. *Winter Science Activities*. New York: Holiday House, 1966.

Index

ailanthus, 34
American sycamore tree, 33
ant, 20–21
aphid, 20

basalt, 13, 14
bedrock, 59
bee, 20, 49
beech tree, 34
beetle, 19
birch tree, 34
birds, 36, 37–42, 51–52, 54, 56
blackbird, 41
blue jay, 41
buckhorn, 25
buds, 49, 54
butterfly, 19

cat, 45–46
catbird, 41
caterpillar, 18–19
centipede, 22
cherry tree, 34
chickadee, 41
chickweed, 25
cockroach, 20
cocoons, 19, 53

conglomerate, 13, 14
crabgrass, 25
cricket, 20, 51
crow, 41

daddy longlegs, 22
dandelion, 23, 25, 49
dog, 43, 45

earthworm, 15, 22, 53
eggs, insect, 17, 53, 54
erosion, 10
evergreen trees, 53
excavation, 59–60
experiments, 7, 9–10, 11, 29–30, 49–57

fall, activities for, 53–54
fern, 27
flower, 25–26, 49, 54
    pollination, 25–26, 49
fly, 20
fossil, 60

ginkgo tree, 33–34
glacier, 12
gneiss, 13, 14
granite, 12–13, 14